Blockchain: Inter Transaction

A Handbook for Blockchain Beginners

Dipender Bhamrah
Gursimran Jit Oberoi

BPB PUBLICATIONS

First Edition 2018

Copyright © BPB Publications, INDIA

ISBN: 978-93-8655-196-2

Distributors:

BPB PUBLICATIONS
20, Ansari Road, Darya Ganj
New Delhi 110002
Ph: 23254990/23254991

COMPUTER BOOK CENTRE
12, Shrungar Shopping Centre,
M.G.Road, BENGALURU–560001
Ph: 25587923/25584641

MICRO MEDIA
Shop No. 5, Mahendra Chambers, 150 DN
Rd. Next to Capital Cinema, V.T. (C.S.T.)
Station, MUMBAI-400 001
Ph: 22078296/22078297

BPB BOOK CENTRE
376 Old Lajpat Rai Market,
Delhi-110006
Ph: 23861747

DECCAN AGENCIES
4-3-329, Bank Street,
Hyderabad-500195
Ph: 24756967/24756400

Published by Manish Jain for BPB Publications, 20, Ansari Road, Darya Ganj, New Delhi-110002 and Printed by Repro India Pvt Ltd, Mumbai

Table of Contents

Setting the Context

Blockchain and Bitcoins, nowadays are the talk of the town. It is the next big wave after the internet. This book, 'Internet of Transactions' is named to indicate the open and public systems for transactions. Just as anybody do not prove their identity to anywhere for using the Internet, this system does it for transactions.

When I started my research with my friend and co-author of this book, I had some difficulty about knowing where to start from. There were a plethora of articles about blockchain and it was hard to find a starting point. Some were too technical and some were too generic, And this is the reason why we wrote this book.

If you see yourself as someone who understands computers (like excel), you should be good to go. The book is a good read for the:

- People who are starting to learn blockchain.
- Technical Managers.
- Someone who wants to develop a conceptual understanding on the subject.
- Naive investors in this field.

We have made an effort to ensure that there are no deep jargons, and if any, are simplified for understanding, such that a person with some understanding of computers can understand. The book will not leave you puzzled, but will encourage you to learn more and explore the area. This book will definitely not take you into technical details or take a systems or coding approach. It will set you ready, so that when you read some articles, news or participate in discussions or investing opportunities, you have the understanding of how it works and what it can do for you, your business, the organizations and for the society.

Introduction - A brief history

Technology is the heart of everything we do these days - good or bad. It empowers humans to value or violate each other's right (such as privacy), in profound new ways.

One such revolution, that we are experiencing and yet to experience it in full force is the '*blockchain*' system. Going back in time, cryptographically secured chain of blocks were described in the 90's as a first work in this field. This research was a result of the insecurities to transact securely, with a credit card over the internet. However, following the financial debacle in 2008, the work of secured chain of blocks came into notice in about 2008, when a *pseudo* character named, *Satoshi Nakamoto*, published open whitepapers about blockchain and digital currency. This digital currency, known as Bitcoin, it uses blockchain system as a core component of the way it handles the transactions.

However, *Satoshi Nakamoto* used the terms *block & chain* separately in his whitepaper in 2008. It was only in 2016, when the terms *block & chain* came into a single word '*blockchain*', which is now being viewed with great potential across different domains.

In early 2017, the *Harvard Business Review* suggested that blockchain is a foundational technology and thus "has the potential to create new foundations for our economic and social systems."

Foundational Concepts of a Blockchain System

The *blockchain* system, has provided us a secure global platform to perform transactions over the internet (some call it the Trust Protocol!). What Internet did to Communication, *Blockchain* has done to the way we do the transactions, and hence I named this book as the *Internet of Transactions*. While the technology behind *blockchain* is a bit complicated to dive deep into it, but the concept in itself is simple to understand. Today, big organizations & governments are exploring the use of *blockchains*, to revolutionize the way information is stored and transactions occur, to make their systems more cost efficient, fast, secure, automated and practically hack-proof. These models, however, not necessarily involve any cryptocurrencies (such as *Bitcoin*), but they will use the *blockchain* system for improving transaction handling. Such is the power and potential of this system.

A grand vision which was initially meant only for the financial system, by a pseudo character (*Satoshi*), has stunned the world by its simplicity and how it can be replicated to other areas of society, organizations and individuals. Here, we shall discuss the design principles of this system, which are derived, and were never explicitly mentioned by the inventor. These principles, will help a new diver to understand the concept at a higher level, before digging in.

Honesty

The system is designed in such a manner that any person, who is transacting in this system can trust it, due to the procedures imbibed into it. Even if there is a case of someone not acting honestly, the system makes it practically impossible to act in that manner, due to the cost & resource requirements. It also tackles the problem of *double spending*, a common problem in the online world. Double spending essentially means a person A, who has 100 units, promises to pay 80 units each to Person B and Person C. But, the problem here is that this Person A is trying to give more money that he actually has, spending an amount of 80 units twice, to pay Person B & Person C. In this, each transaction is timestamped which helps it to behave in an honest way.

Another way in which honesty is built into the system is that the ledger is practically *immutable*. (Although no ledger is truly immutable). This means that once a transaction has been entered into the blockchain system and verified, it cannot be reversed, edited or deleted. And once you know that it cannot be altered, you will trust the system. Any chances of forgery and frauds will be eliminated.

Transparency

Building honesty requires transparency as a prerequisite. All transactions in a blockchain are available to everyone who is a part of the system. So, if you put your money in a bank, you do not see, where your money goes. However, with the blockchain system in place, backdoor dealings or under-the-table transactions are no more possible due to distributed ledgers. All nodes (people), who are a part of the system, have a copy of the ledger, containing all the transactions. Every action or transaction is passed through a verification process which involves *popular consensus* (will be discussed further) and no central third party or central server stores it.

Decentralized Power

Decentralization in blockchain is achieved in many ways. For a start, there is no single server or authority which controls everything. There are multiple servers setup in the system (nodes), which exists in different locations. Each one of them has a distributed ledger and maintains all the data. As a result of this, the system becomes hack-proof, practically. However, theoretically, the system can still be hacked.

The blockchain system is based on consensus algorithm, which again is based on the design principle of decentralization (of power). So, any change in the transaction data, requires verification. This is where the consensus algorithm comes into picture. If a majority of peers in the system, approve the transaction, then it can be done. However, imagine, if you make a change in the transaction (with the intention to cheat someone), it has to get approved by more than 50% people present in the network around the globe, which you have to influence in a very less time (less than 10 minutes). The mechanism is termed as a *51% attack*, which is near to impossible and makes it practically hack-proof.

When we say that the majority of peers have to agree and approve the transaction, the system also requires them to submit a *proof-of-work.* . These people, are special users termed as *miners*, who get to solve a complex puzzle, which involves a lot of *computational work* to verify this transactional block. They are rewarded by some units (like a bitcoin), if successful, which is their incentive to spend resources at this work.

Note: For a bitcoin blockchain, this is done once in every 10 minutes. And the reward is currently set to 12.5 Bitcoins, which gets halved after every 4 years). So, considering the current value of bitcoin, imagine that in every 10 minutes, someone in this world receives 12.5 bitcoins. This is huge money and a good enough reward to put an effort.

It has to be noted here that, proof-of-work is a concept associated with Bitcoin Blockchain, while different blockchains may use different algorithms. The other popular blockchain, the *Etherium blockchain* is set to use the *proof-of-stake* mechanism by next year.

Security & Privacy

This design principle is also imbibed into the network, like others. The network is secure in itself and is hack-proof. In Spite of our data being available to everyone publicly, it is still impossible for anyone to track who has performed a transaction or who holds what amount of unit value. Each user's identity is hidden in the ledger by the use of some special functions, which the user only knows (*private key cryptography*). Therefore, anonymity is another form of security, which is coded into this system. This is ensured by cryptographic functions and hashing algorithms. The system does not require your email address, or name to be associated with your transactions. Therefore, problems such as identity theft, frauds, ransomware, etc. will not exist anymore, which is a big pain point and a challenge in today's world.

Imagine, if you can control and monetize your own data. So, if a company requires your age, gender and certain preferences to be available to them, you can sell it to them, without sharing other sensitive details, and they pay you for this.

Inclusivity

Governments and organizations try hard to include maximum people into their systems, be it a financial inclusion, any government scheme or any such other activity. Therefore, we can conclude that any system which includes more and more people into it, will be powerful and empowers them to drives more people into it. The blockchain system was design by Satoshi Nakamoto, which could work even without the internet and by using a basic phone, which drastically lowers the entry barriers of technical knowledge, economic state or coverage issues. It also empowers people by eliminating third parties which control us and act as aggregators. The blockchain systems threaten to eliminate the Uber's and Airbnb's of the world. Instead, it gives control to people who interact with one another to exchange value through transactions. Eliminating third parties also means lowering down the cost of transactions. Consider sending money to someone outside your country and how much fee you pay as the transaction fee. This is completely eliminated in blockchain as it is an optional criteria.

Now that we understand these five foundational elements (*their applications explained in Use Case section*) of the blockchain system, it will be much easier to go a bit deep into the system and understand at a slightly technical level. You must now understand how the system works and the various mechanisms that enable these foundational principles.

Introducing Blockchain

Transactions are a very important part of any business and keeping their records, traceability is even more important. The past transactions of any person or organization reveal a lot about its performance and also its future planning (thanks to predictive analytics). Although many companies maintain a record of these transactions, they are still confined to that organization only. These transactions are not visible to the customers of the organization. Some organizations use software to maintain while others still do it manually, which is prone to errors. However, blockchain claims to solve these problems.

In a very simple term, it is a set of rules (protocols), based on a growing number of ledgers (like in a bank), called blockchains, which consists of a chain of blocks, each block containing a set of encrypted transactions. It enables to transact with one another (Peer to Peer) without involving a third party.

I assume that you understand a basic excel sheet. Consider an excel sheet as a ledger with some transactions or stored data, which is shared (or *public*) within the team of 6 members, such that each one of you has a copy of that on your system. This ledger has some columns (like timestamp, user ID, etc.), for data regarding transactions to be stored. We will discuss about the transactions with the example later in the book. This excel sheet can be accessed by all, even to those who are not a part of this group, which means it is *public*. But people do not know, who has done a particular transaction (refers to the row of the sheet), because the way your user ID is written (it is *encrypted*). Now, let's assume that a sheet can hold a maximum of 1,000 rows. So, as soon as the 1,000 rows are filled up with transactions, a new spreadsheet is created, which points to the previous spreadsheet, thus forming a *chain*. This sheet is updated after an interval of time, say 10 minutes, during which the transactions are *verified* and linked to previous sheet. The sheets in the example, are blocks and the complete system is known as blockchain. This should give you an overview how the system works.

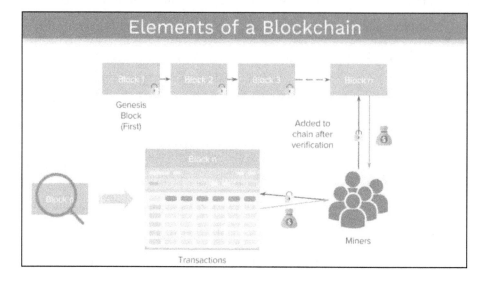

This technology has a great potential use cases, and some people and organizations have just begun to realize. Many smart & influential people have quit their jobs to explore this space. The U.S. government set up a 7 member committee, to discuss how Bitcoin can be regulated, to stop its misuse. It was about a year after that time, when *Ben Lawsky*, quit his job as the superintendent of financial services for the New York state build an advisory firm in this area. In 2014, *J.P.Morgan*'s *Paul Camp*, who formerly held the title of global head and managing director at *JPMorgan*'s transactions services unit, joined as a corporate treasurer and executive vice president of financial operations as well as CFO at a Startup in this field. *Blythe Masters*, CFO at *J.P.Morgan*'s Investment Bank launched a blockchain based startup too. In November 2017, even the *State Bank of India*, India's largest Public Sector bank has announced that it is ready to test blockchain based transactions in a month or so. There are many more examples of such influential personalities & organizations exploring this technology, which adds to confidence.

Like every technology, Blockchain also has its downsides and has been misused already, making people and organizations wary of adopting this. Due to the anonymity of its users, it has already been used to sell illegal drugs, weapons & child pronography. However, tweaking it a bit, these problems are tackled. Although, cryptocurrencies are still unregulated in some countries like India (Bitcoin is not approved by Reserve Bank of India), Russia, Japan, US and several others, some governments are exploring and investing in it. Switzerland is a major hub of blockchain innovation as the biggest disruption is to financial sector. However, for India, the Reserve Bank of India has already floated whitepapers and not leaving Bitcoin & blockchain out of its purview.

Definition

Blockchain is the spine of the Bitcoin currency. This system is now being replicated across many areas due to the advantages that we have discussed in the previous sections.

Blockchain is a publicly distributed database, which holds the encrypted ledger.

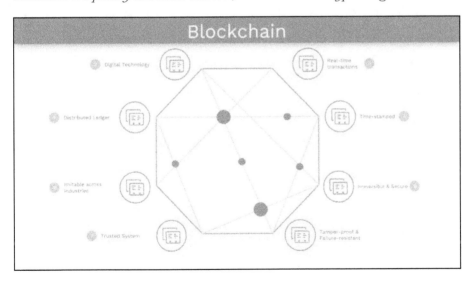

"The blockchain is an incorruptible digital ledger of economic transactions that can be programmed to record not just financial transactions but virtually everything of value."

– Don & Alex *Tapscott*, authors Blockchain Revolution (2016)

The word 'blockchain' comes from the chain of blocks that are created. A block is a collection of all recently occurred transactions that have been verified. Once a transaction is completed, it is *hashed* (encrypted) and stored in a block. Then this transaction is verified and all such grouped transactions are combined in a block, which becomes a part of the chain. This chain contains all the blocks since the beginning of this blockchain. This chain keeps on growing with time and it is estimated a new block is added in every 10 minutes.

"As revolutionary as it sounds, Blockchain truly is a mechanism to bring everyone to the highest degree of accountability. No more missed transactions, human or machine errors, or even an exchange that was not done with the consent of the parties involved. Above anything else, the most critical area where Blockchain helps is to guarantee the validity of a transaction by recording it not only on a main register but a connected distributed system of registers, all of which are connected through a secure validation mechanism."

—Ian Khan, TEDx Speaker | Author | Technology Futurist

"Blockchain solves the problem of manipulation. When I speak about it in the West, people say they trust Google, Facebook, or their banks. But the rest of the world doesn't trust organizations and corporations that much — I mean Africa, India, the Eastern Europe, or Russia. It's not about the places where people are really rich. Blockchain's opportunities are the highest in the countries that haven't reached that level yet."

—Vitalik Buterin, inventor of Ethereum

Types of Blockchain

Blockchain, when invented as a part of the Bitcoin currency, was public in nature. This means that it is available to everyone and anyone. However, as we move forward, many institutions like banks and governments realized that they could use a permissioned blockchain within their organization to use its benefits, where the validator is a member of the organization. Therefore, based on the uses, blockchains is categorized into three types.

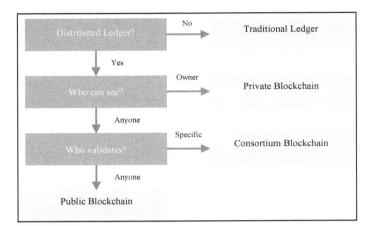

❖ Public Blockchains

These blockchains are open source and no one needs permission to participate in them (known as *permission less*). Anyone can download the code of the blockchain and start on their local machine. The transactions, which form the blocks, are then publicly and openly available to explore and analyses. The focus or the impact of a public blockchain is disruption and innovation.

Some examples of the famous public blockchains are Bitcoin and Etherium.

❖ Consortium Blockchains

When many organizations come together to form a consortium, and use the blockchain to restrict the participants transacting in the blockchain, it is known as a consortium blockchain. This kind of a blockchain enables public to read the database but not transact inside it. The people who are allowed by the group of organizations to be a part of the blockchain, are only allowed to transact. The focus or the impact of a public blockchain is innovation and disruption, and has transaction approval frequency of around 10 minutes.

A common example may be a set of 10 banking institutions of a country coming together and coming to a consensus that of all 10 or 8 verify each block then the block is considered as valid. The members who are allowed by these banks to be a part of this chain can only transact in this, while it is open to public to view.

❖ Private Blockchains

Here, the write permissions for verification process are restricted to only one organization. However, people can still read (optional) the transactions. This may include applications within a company such as database management. This type of blockchain uses the concept of blockchain to benefit from its features like reducing transaction costs, replacing legacy systems to simplify processes and remove data redundancies. The key impact of a private blockchain is similar to a consortium blockchain, which is cost-cutting and has shorter transaction approval frequency (around 100 milliseconds) as compared to public blockchains (which is 10 minutes).

The distinctions stated above are very broad and still have to be matured, considering that this technology is in very early stages.

Key Terminology

Now that you understand the concepts and the foundations of a blockchain system, it is the right time to know some of the key terms used in the blockchain system. These terms are frequently used, no matter if you read, discuss or dive technical into it.

Mining

Mining is the process of extracting value from the blockchain. This value can be in various kinds of units, such as Bitcoins or anything else. The primary purpose of mining is to enable the blockchain to reach a tamper-proof consensus. And the consensus can be reached if more number of miners exist, which make the network more secure and less vulnerable to attack.

Every block (a collection of transactions), which is created on the blockchain network, needs to be verified before being added to the main blockchain. Some participants on the blockchain search and find *unverified* blocks of recent transactions and broadcast it to all the nodes to confirm for validity and truthfulness of the transaction. These participants are called *miners*.

If the transactions are validated by all the nodes and considered as passed by the blockchain, the miners are rewarded for their effort. Their effort is rewarded in two ways:

1. **Block Rewards:** If a miner finds any recent unverified block, the block has a fixed reward attached to it, which is given to *miner*. Block Rewards are decided by a *block schedule* and change according to a set formula after a certain period of time.

2. **Transaction Fee:** The transaction can have some transaction fee attached to it, to incentivize the miner additionally and is an optional feature of the blockchain.

The *miners* are eligible for the above discussed rewards only if they meet certain conditions. The fulfilment of these conditions is known as *Proof of Work* and shall be discussed in the next section.

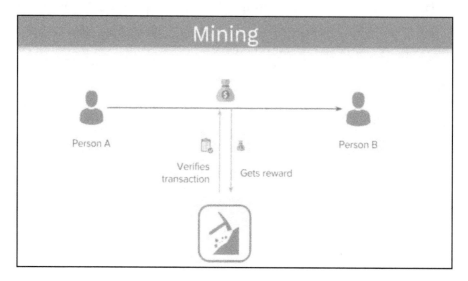

Taking the example of the bitcoin blockchain, if you were to mine a bitcoin in 2009, you were paid 50 bitcoins for each verified block on the blockchain. As of November 2017, a miner will receive 12.5 bitcoins for verifying each block of transactions. According to the block schedule calculations, the last bitcoin is supposed to be mined in the year 2140. After all the bitcoins are mined, the miners will make bitcoin from the transaction fee included on the blockchain.

Date reached	Block	Reward Era	BTC/ block	Year (estimate)	Start BTC	BTC Added	End BTC	BTC Increase	End BTC % of Limit
2009-01-03	0	1	50.00	2009	0	2625000	2625000	infinite	12.500%
2010-04-22	52500	1	50.00	2010	2625000	2625000	5250000	100.00%	25.000%
2011-01-28	105000	1	50.00	2011*	5250000	2625000	7875000	50.00%	37.500%
2011-12-14	157500	1	50.00	2012	7875000	2625000	10500000	33.33%	50.000%
2012-11-28	210000	2	25.00	2013	10500000	1312500	11812500	12.50%	56.250%
2013-10-09	262500	2	25.00	2014	11812500	1312500	13125000	11.11%	62.500%

2014-08-11	315000	2	25.00	2015	13125000	1312500	14437500	10.00%	68.750%
2015-07-29	367500	2	25.00	2016	14437500	1312500	15750000	9.09%	75.000%
2016-07-09	420000	3	12.50	2016	15750000	656250	16406250	4.17%	78.125%
2017-06-23	472500	3	12.50	2018	16406250	656250	17062500	4.00%	81.250%
	525000	3	12.50	2019	17062500	656250	17718750	3.85%	84.375%
	577500	3	12.50	2020	17718750	656250	18375000	3.70%	87.500%
	630000	4	6.25	2021	18375000	328125	18703125	1.79%	89.063%
	682500	4	6.25	2022	18703125	328125	19031250	1.75%	90.625%
	735000	4	6.25	2023	19031250	328125	19359375	1.72%	92.188%
	787500	4	6.25	2024	19359375	328125	19687500	1.69%	93.750%

Bitcoin Block Schedule - **Ref:** https://en.bitcoin.it/wiki/Controlled_supply

But can you mine a block on a laptop today, as was possible in 2008?

The answer is NO. The reason is: increasing in number of miners. As the number of miners increase, the task of mining is made more difficult. The concept of increasing the difficulty and how it is done is discussed in the *Hashing* section.

A simple laptop or desktop computer does not have enough computing power to act as an economically viable *mining node* for a reward (say a bitcoin). This is because the electricity cost of mining that fraction of a bitcoin is far more than the amount of bitcoin earned by the owner, using such computational power. The efficiency of the miner is known by the *hashing rate* the miner node possesses. *Hash rate* is the number of hash functions a node can perform for a certain blockchain. (You may refer to *Hashing* section also)

Mining is currently carried out using the following hardware:

1. **CPU:** This is highly inefficient for major bitcoins. Maybe profitable for mining some new cryptocurrencies

2. **GPU:** Basically, these are dedicated graphics cards which are more efficient than a CPU processor but consumes more energy.

3. **ASIC (Application Specific Integrated Circuit):** An integrated circuit designed specifically to carry out one and only one function. In this case, the machine maximizes hash rate at the lowest energy cost.

Since it is very difficult for a node or machine to mine bitcoins on its own, sometimes people pool their hash power to a single node and share the reward. This is known as *pool mining*. As a closing thought, miners are critical to the success of any blockchain as they make the blockchain more fair, stable, safer and more secure.

Cryptography and Digital Signatures

Blockchain uses Private Key Cryptography to secure identities and hash functions to make blockchain immutable. The hashing algorithms are so precise and complex that the decryption and encryption are virtually impossible to crack through.

There are two kinds of keys, public & private. Public keys are seen by everyone on the network, while private key is only known to the node to which it belongs. Each user in the system is known by a 'pseudo' name, which is public to everyone (called the *public verification key* for digital signatures). At the same time, each user also has a signing key (called the *private verification key* for digital signatures), which is only known to that user.

The problem with a public key is that it is known to everyone and can be intercepted with a hacker. So, if A is sending some information to B, then if A announces its *public key* than any other hacker in the system may also forge this transaction. The solution to this is a *private key*. So, when A sends the information to B, it signs the data with its *private key* (called *hashing*, which explained in next section) and sends it across. When B receives the data, it decrypts the data and matches the value to confirm if the received data is correct or not.

This is just a brief description of the concept and we have deliberately not dived deep into the technical know-how of the concept of cryptography.

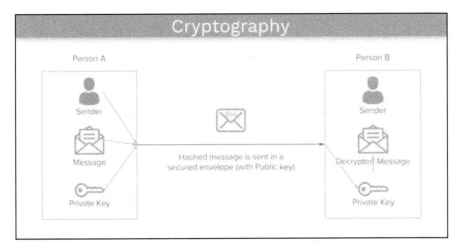

Hashing

Hashing is a technique to convert any function that can be used to map data of arbitrary size to data of fixed size. The function which is used to perform this computation is called a **hash function**. When a user sends a message to another user over a network, a hash of the intended message is generated and encrypted by using a hash function, and is sent along with the message. The result of the hash is known as a *digest or hash*. When the message (*digest*) is received, the receiver decrypts the hash as well as the message. Then, the receiver creates another hash from the message. If the two hashes (received and created) are identical when compared, then it can be said that a secure transmission has occurred and the message has been correctly received. This hashing process ensures that the message is not altered by an unauthorized end user. Some of the famous cryptographic hash functions are MD5, SHA-256 or so on. The digest obtained is very complex and is obtained after complex computations. In a bitcoin blockchain, the leading number of zeros in the digest, determine the level of difficulty of finding the right digest.

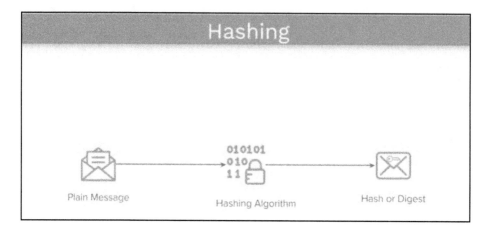

Hashing is *collision resistant*, which simply means that for two distinct inputs, it is extremely hard to find an identical output. It is hard in terms of the time and effort required to do so, and the protocol should be so strong that it takes astronomically long time to discover a colliding input for the same output. Also, the hash function hides all contexts of the input. By this, we mean that, while it should not be possible to say that was the number as input (let's say a number was used as input), but whether that number is odd or even, should also not be discoverable.

P2P Network

In the absence of any centralized third party, Peer to Peer networks ensure that there is complete consistency with the distributed ledgers. As explained earlier, a person who wants to send some units to another person in the blockchain, propagates it in the network, which is a P2P network. Also, if one person tries to make slight change in the transaction (with all the required resources), still, his copy of the ledger will not be reflected in the blockchain because most people in the network who have the original block will reject the change. If someone tries to change an existing block, it can only be done by producing all blocks in the chain, which is near to impossible and hence this method secures the blockchain.

The blockchain P2P network is based on consensus algorithms. This means that when a majority, or say more than 50% of the participants of the blockchain, agree to a certain decision, then that decision is validated.

Different blockchains use different consensus algorithms. The Bitcoin blockchain uses the Proof-of-Work concept while the other blockchains use Proof-of-Stake and other mechanisms. We shall discuss this concept in detail in the next section and also compare it with other popular mechanisms.

Proof-of-Work

One of the primary goals of the blockchain is to reach consensus on the network through nodes which are rewarded for acting fairly and honestly.

If blockchain was a business owner and wanted to get the job (of consensus) done from several workers (miners), how would it find out, how much to pay to each person? Also, wouldn't it want to ensure that the hardest working contributor would be prioritized and rewarded first? What if, the job was so simple that even the laziest worker would claim a reward without even working for it? The challenge was to create a system which rewards the miners fairly and is one of the crucial decisions, the blockchain algorithm has to make and is ably solved by a *proof-of-work* mechanism.

The blockchain releases the block rewards only to miners which submit a *valid* proof of work. Without a valid proof of work, cheater nodes may try to overrun the system with their own set of transactions, try to validate them and tear down the integrity of the blockchain. A good example of an attack resistant blockchain is DDOS. This *proof of work is a computational puzzle* which the mining node must solve successfully in order to submit a valid, previously unverified block on the blockchain and be rewarded for it. The solution to this computational problem is considered as a valid *proof of work*. The solver attaches a hashed code, called digest to the transaction as a proof of work.

(You may refer *hashing* section or *An Example of a Blockchain Transaction* section for more details).

But if everyone solves the problem, what could the blockchain do? A blockchain, like bitcoin, is capable of adding a block in every 10 minutes. Then how do we ensure that miners submit only one block in every 10 minutes?

The answer is to this is *difficulty*. The 'difficulty' of the computational puzzle given to the miners changes itself according to the number of miners on the network and the demand on the network. Difficulty calibration happens after every 2016 blocks, which is approximately two weeks on the blockchain network (considering 1 block in every 10 minutes).

To understand, you may visualize the '*difficulty*' as a *Sudoku puzzle*. Let's assume that the blockchain wants to make the miners solve a 3x3 sudoku in the beginning. After two weeks, with a lot more miners on the network, we need to increase the difficulty. So now the network will want the miners to solve a 4x4 puzzle to ensure that in every 10 minutes, only 1 block is submitted to the blockchain. This can be scaled up to a 100x100 sudoku. But what truly makes this concept great is that even though the puzzle is now exponentially difficult to solve, the difficulty for the network to see whether the puzzle was solved correctly did not change much. This asymmetry makes any *proof of work* function really special.

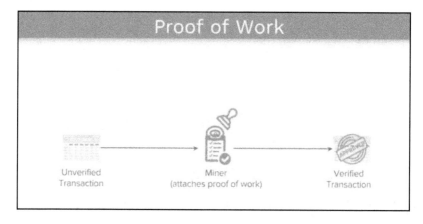

More the number of mining nodes, more secure and resistant the network will become to outside attacks. But now some nodes will have to wait longer than others to get rewarded and their effort will simply become unprofitable due to the costs incurred. These unprofitable nodes will have to shut down, upgrade their hardware or mine on another blockchain to survive, where their Return on Investment still makes sense.

As every technology has some disadvantage, following are some of the major drawbacks of the Proof of Work algorithm,

1. **51% attack:** If a single miner or a group of miners can generate more than 51% of the total block validations for a blockchain, they can halt an honest transaction and choose to verify another transaction, which will benefit them. The cost of such an attack is enormous and is only hypothetical at the moment. As of Nov, '17, miners would need hardware worth of 3 billion dollars and an electricity cost of $5.6 million/day to carry out such an attack on the bitcoin blockchain.

2. **Consumption of Energy:** The energy consumed by the miners to mine the reward, costs extremely high and is considered as a waste of energy by many experts

The proposed solution to the *51% attack* vulnerability is a *Proof of Stake (POS)* algorithm. A proof of stake algorithm attributes only as much percentage of mining power (or hash power) to the node (or miner) as it holds some percentage of cryptocurrency. This helps to solve the above two problems:

To carry out a 51% attack, miner would have to literally own 51% of the rewards in the ecosystem. The cost of mounting this attack would be even more as compared to a hypothetical PoW 51% attack.

There is no need for expensive mining setups now which take up lots of energy. A miner can simply buy rewards (such as bitcoins) and request to mine the network by staking its reward with the network. This will solve the ecological problem usually associated with mining on a PoW algorithm

An Example of a Blockchain Transaction

Let us take an example where 6 people are a part of the blockchain network. Each of the 6 people, Person A, Person B, Person C, Person D, Person E & Person F, have certain account balances and Person D & Person E are *special users* (called *miners*). Account balances are never stored explicitly in a bitcoin blockchain, but are derived by using the blockchain transactions ever recorded. (However, Ethereum blockchain stores the account balances.)

Note: To keep it generic, I will use the term 'units' which can be taken as any unit based on the domain in which blockchain is to be applied.

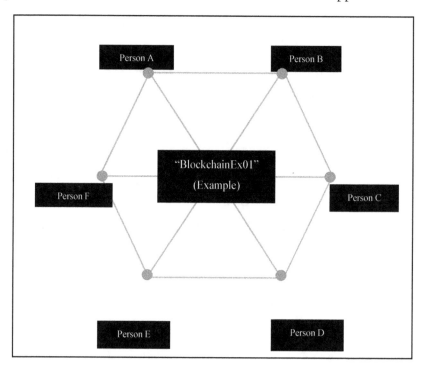

Here is a record of their account balances for our understanding only (which is not maintained in a bitcoin blockchain). We have understood earlier, how these units are earned by these participants. If you cannot recall how have they earned these units, we will touch upon them again.

Participant	Account Balance
Person A	100 units
Person B	100 units
Person C	150 units
Person D (miner)	50 units
Person E (miner)	100 units
Person F	150 units

Assumptions for simplified understanding:

- We will treat Excel as our ledger.

- An excel worksheet with the name 'BlockchainEx01' is our blockchain for the example.

- Each sheet within the worksheet represents a block of information.

- Each block can have maximum of 10 records, which represents 10 rows in an excel sheet.

Now, Person A wants to transfer 90 units to Person B. So, Person A uses a set of information (explained below) and broadcasts his request to all the other 5 people in the blockchain to reduce his account balance by 90 units & increase Person B's balance by the same amount.

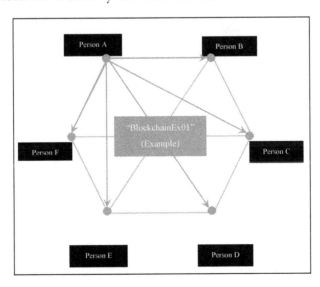

The transaction in the ledger will look something like this (showing only some part).

Previous Block No.	NULL					
Timestamp	From User	To User	Units_Transferred	Units_Retained	Units_Fee (Optional)	
20171030 110028 hrs	04659fhworbdijci12nvod	64910dhqocbdusi73idos	10	89	1	

The initial part of the transaction block "Block01" is explained as below:

In our example, a string under *'From User'* is the *public key* for Person A, and the string under *'To User'* is the *public key* for Person B. When Person A sends the above data, it is digitally signed by using its own *private key*, which is not shown here.

Also, you can notice a *"Units Fee"* column, which is completely optional in the blockchain system. Person A may or may not incentivize anyone with a transaction fee.

Note: Transaction fee may be used to invite miners to quickly verify their transaction, giving them this extra incentive.

The remaining part of the transaction are as below:

Challenge	ProofofWork	Chain of Ownership	Digest
lapfu04wiskq		[Digest01], [Digest02], [Digest03]	[Digest04]

Now, when Person A sends 90 units to Person B, a *'chain of ownership'* (for our understanding only) is also attached in the transaction detail, which proves that Person A, had received those units from previous owners and now has sufficient balance to transfer it to Person B. These previous transaction details are not included in the transaction in its complete form, but the details are hashed and their result, a *digest*, is only attached to it (Refer to 'Hashing' section for more details). So, in our example, if Person A has 3 verified transactions earlier, 3 digests are attached in this transaction. Also, under *Digest*, this transaction hashed or encrypted result is also sent.

Now, the transaction is first verified by the miners Person D & Person E, who check that if Person A has the required balance or not and also if he has not committed the same to another Person (to avoid *double spending*). As we had discussed earlier, Person D & Person E are special users called *miners*. Verification of a transaction is not an easy task and requires complex mathematical computations & security implementations to do this. You may think that Person B may also do the same job, knowing everything, given the digest of all previous transactions, but what Person B does not know is that if Person A has promised another Person F to give 90 units. So, these miners, verify the double-spending problem, using the *timestamp* of Person A's all transactions (which are public). They solve a *challenge* thrown to them to verify the transaction.

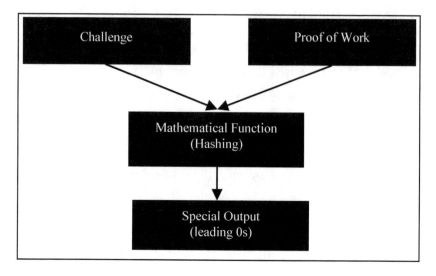

So, when the challenge & proof of work are hashed together, and the result is a *special output* with a fixed number of leading zeros, say 40 for a blockchain, the puzzle is said to be solved. Miners try different set of 'proof-of-work' strings (based on probability) such that when they are hashed with the challenge, a special output comes, where the first 40 bits are zeros. The leading number of zeros control the difficulty with which this puzzle can be solved and increasing each leading zero doubles the computational effort for the miners and making it hard to solve the puzzle.

Once the transaction is verified, a miner attaches his '*proof-of-work*' to the transaction and marks the transaction as verified. Person B, who is the receiver, checks if the transaction was verified (using proof-of-work), and accepts the transfer.

Then, the digests of all such recent transactions get added to this block, which is again hashed, and becomes a part of the chain of all such blocks. The ledger copy is updated for everyone else in the blockchain. So, we are not dealing with an isolated block of transaction here but a chain of blocks.

A Bit More about Blockchain

Now that you have the basic understanding of a blockchain, more so with respect to a bitcoin blockchain, it is almost essential to know some of the advanced concepts used in other blockchains.

Smart Contract

Imagine a traveler who wants to buy a travel insurance policy. If the baggage is lost in transit, the person goes to the airline office and initiates a refund after filing relevant documents. Apart from the bad experience to the customer, this takes a lot of effort and time.

Now, imagine a computer program is created, which has the function of self-execution, in case of meeting certain criteria. In the above case, if a travel insurance program were to run which would have all prior information of the traveler and the airline, all relevant documents and banking connections set up and uploaded and this program is directed to release the payment to the passenger as soon as it reads baggage lost trigger from the airline's software, it would lead to massive cost savings for the airline, insurer and the passenger. This, in simple terms, is a self-executing *smart contract*.

A smart contract is a protocol which can auto execute, facilitate, verify or enforce the negotiation of a contract. Smart Contracts were first proposed by Nick Szabo in 1996. They save time and money, prevent collusion, enforce censorship and counterparty risk and have a long range of use cases in every industry.

Currently smart contracts are being used and promoted primarily by the cryptocurrency space. They not only fulfil the classic use cases of a contract but are now implemented in general purpose programming.

A great early use case for smart contracts is formation of foundations and projects with key goals, functionalities and scope written into an open source smart contract. This smart contract can then raise funds for the foundation to complete a certain objective. All the *initial coin offerings* (ICOs) are crowd fundraising events and are happening with the help of smart contracts.

Note: An ICO is very similar to an IPO (Initial Public Offering).

Major work on smart contract layer was done by the Ethereum foundation. They were the first ones to fully visualize and develop a layer of smart contracts on the top of basic blockchain. This enabled the development of Decentralized Applications or popularly known as DApps, which has further extended the use cases of a decentralized economy. For example, Decentralized Stock exchanges, Decentralized eMail, Internet etc.

Vitalik Buterin is the brainchild behind launching the Ethereum smart contract execution and DApps and is also pioneering the proof of stake consensus algorithm for the Ethereum Foundation. He is widely considered by many as the brightest brain in the community in Cryptoeconomics.

Cryptoeconomics

Cryptoeconomics is NOT the study of effects of cryptocurrency on economic activities. It is an endeavor more comparable to Mechanism Design. Mechanism design is a field which utilizes economics and game theory concepts to reverse engineer solutions to a given set of machine language problems. For example, design incentives and penalties in a system so that all the players in the system act fairly or are otherwise penalized for bad behavior.

Game theory studies the interaction of peers and competing parties in a situation and understands the best strategic outcome for each player in every scenario individually and as a group. The problem Cryptoeconomics is to solve, how to keep a decentralized P2P network running fairly, despite attempts from adversaries to disrupt the network. And how well does a network recover from such an attack?

It is generally referred to as a *Byzantine Generals Problem*. The problem was proposed by Leslie Lamport, Robert Shostak and Marshall Pease in a paper of the same name in 1982. The problem was initially proposed to explore how a system would handle conflicting or bad information being received at its end and how to ensure that only correct outcomes are executed.

The problem is described as a group of generals who have surrounded a city and are in control of their posts. They can either attack the city or retreat. But they are unaware of the actions of the other generals. The problem is compounded by the fact that some generals may be traitors and are sending out different calls action to different generals. This may result in an unfavorable outcome of some generals retreating and some advancing at the same time. In such a case, outcome of a total attack or a total retreat, would be much better than actions of a split-up army.

A working solution to this problem already had applications in the fields of computer science and logic, biology, politics, economics, business and philosophy. But what about the Peer to Peer systems?

So, how does a system wants to achieve *trustlessness* from a third party, by ensuringthat its own participants will act in a fair manner?

Satoshi Nakamoto is practically the first person (or a group of persons) to successfully design a solution to the *Byzantine Generals Problem* and implement it to a Peer to Peer system. P2P systems have existed before in torrent networks, but there was no economic incentive to stay within the networks to stay honest hence they never truly went mainstream.

The linking of *proof of work* mechanism with smartly programmed economic incentive was the final piece of the puzzle needed for the blockchain to create and retain valid consensus among the miners. Now there is more incentive for a miner to send true data on the chain instead of trying to send false data and the cost of such an act would be high for a miner, higher than the expected reward of cheating. Now, the honest data could be shared among participants with known confidence that each data set is valid and true, without the need for a third party to validate it. This form of trustlessness set *Bitcoin* apart from every P2P technology out there and making it truly transparent and free from control of bad actors. This gives more credibility and stability to a system in the long run.

Blockchains in fact is just one of the use cases for the Cryptoeconomics and this field is just in its infancy and constantly evolving as more and more talent joins this field to further its advance. Currently, Cryptoeconomics is being applied to 3 types of systems within the blockchain ecosystem:

- **Consensus Protocols:** Which protocols should we use to create consensus on a blockchain. Proof of Work and Proof Of stake are two iterations that are currently observed and applied on various blockchains as of now, but we may yet see some improved consensus mechanism in a few years.

- **Cryptoeconomics Application Design:** DApps created on the blockchains also need user growth and adoption to survive. A badly designed token metric and prediction algorithms of how actual users will utilize these tokens or how many tokens are required by a blockchain to function smoothly will lead to a definite de-adoption from the network.

- **State Channels:** Scaling transactions on a blockchain is a big hurdle for the programmers and is the foremost problem to solve for the blockchain community. State channels are basically group of off chain transactions which are added to the blockchain after certain stipulated time but not right away. This decreases the direct load on the blockchain to update all the data and moreover, helps the transactions to move faster as they are settled and validated on the off-chain state channels first before being updated on the blockchain. Cryptoeconomics will solve a big part of the puzzle in maintaining consensus on these state channels. 'Lightning network' is one such update which will be implemented on Bitcoin and Litecoin after successful testing.

DApps

DApps stands for *Decentralized Applications*. They are the applications and use cases which sit on the top of the protocol blockchains and enable real time interactions between the final users and a blockchain. A DApp is to a blockchain what any website (like Amazon.com) is to the Internet.

As blockchain may have multiple use cases and applications, it is imperative that it has an ecosystem of well-developed DApps to bring each of these use cases into adoption and improve the society and businesses at large.

Each DApp is programmed according to the rules and limitations of the blockchain on which it will be implemented. An Ethereum DApp can only be programmed in Solidity language. So, any programmer looking to create a DApp on the Ethereum blockchain will have to learn *Solidity* (A programming language).

Some of the salient features of a good DApp are:

1. It has an open source code which can be vetted by the community if need be.

2. It is decentralized.

3. Good token economics and incentives for the participants on the network.

As an example, Ethereum is a blockchain which has a protocol of programmable smart contracts. Since smart contracts have several applications across industries, more than 850 Dapps are currently being developed by using the Ethereum blockchain. Some examples of Ethereum Dapps:

1. **Gnosis:** rediction and market platform

2. **Ethticket:** Buy and sell event tickets

3. **Storj:** Cloud storage

4. **EthLend:** Lending and Credit service

5. **INS:** Direct producer to seller FMCG product marketplace

6. **Crypto Kitties:** Breed and trade digital cats

7. **District Ox:** Decentralized exchange for digital assets

Fork

Often there are changes which are proposed amongst the participants within a blockchain network in terms of how the protocol works. These updates can range from changing the block size of the blockchain to upgrading or modifying the consensus protocol that the blockchain is following. When all the nodes on a blockchain agree to follow the updated protocol, a '*soft fork*' can take place. This soft fork is updated across all nodes, which the updated protocols are followed diligently by all nodes. In some cases, there are protocol updates which are not accepted by the majority. In this case, the proposer can split the existing chain into two, with one chain running with the old protocol and the new chain running with the updated protocol. This event is known as a '*hard fork*'. The nodes can choose on their own what protocol they would like to run. Obviously, the chain with more nodes is considered more secure.

Most famous soft fork will be in the year 2018, when Ethereum will move from a proof of stake consensus to a proof of work consensus with the update called '*Casper*'.

Most famous hard fork was in 2017. The increasing transaction costs and confirmation time gave rose to a few Bitcoin hard forks. Some of the well-known ones are Litecoin, Bitcoin Cash, Bitcoin Gold.

Real World Use Cases & Examples

With the provided basic understanding of the blockchain, we now share a common knowledge that blockchain technology in itself is not *disruptive* in nature, because of the fact that it does not reinvent any business model or brings a new programming language on the table to reduce huge costs. However, given its basic architecture and simplified understanding, it offers a lot that can be done by using it, and hence, serves as the *foundational concept*, upon which many organizations belonging to different domains or governments and society can build and benefit. It could even take one or two, or even three decades to realize its potential to the maximum advantage, but the ones realizing it sooner than others will definitely have the advantage over others. Blockchain has huge potential to be used in many areas. Some of the most popular are briefly explained below:

Banking

The financial sector, so far presents the most popular use of blockchain till date. Although not a bank but *Bitcoin (a currency)* is a famous example which relates to the financial sector. Blockchain threatens to eliminate the role of banks and decentralize the system. Many banks over the world are testing this technology (running PoCs) and/or investing in blockchain based FinTech startups. In India, the State Bank of India is also running a prototype to be under testing, around the time when this book is being written.

Blockchain system can be used in various areas inside the banking domain. While these applications are still under testing, their commercial viability is still not determined. But we are focusing here on the application of blockchain in the banking domain, which are,

1. **Identity:** Banks may simplify their KYC process to verify applicant identity. Banks could also benefit hugely from the blockchain by setting

up a consortium blockchain among the banks of a country, where they share the identity of customers and can verify easily.

2. **Loans:** Blockchain could help to maintain the lifecycle of loan processing, which shall be transparent to the customer. With the shared identity blockchain (discussed above), the banks can also determine credit rating score to see if they can provide loans to a person or organization.

3. **Clearing Transactions & their Settlement:** The most mundane task in the banking sector can also be automated and made efficient by using the blockchain mechanism. In a research, Accenture estimates that America's biggest banks could save up to $10 bn by using blockchain and increasing efficiency into their systems.

While there may be many more areas of application within the banking domain, we have highlighted a few and left to your imagination and further research to explore more into it. Now, let us look at the main benefits of using the blockchain system in banking area:

1. **Cost Cutting:** With the simplification of processes and applying automation using the blockchain, banks are reducing on manpower and their turnaround time to customers.

2. **Efficiency:** The ease and simplicity of maintaining a large database of transactions is the biggest traction point for banks who need to store these transactions in huge databases and follow strict regulatory compliances at the same time.

3. **Innovation:** With the stiff competition from startups in the FinTech area, banks have the opportunity to invest in innovation and lead the change.

Payments & Transfers

The potential for blockchain to disrupt the payments market is out there. Remittances is one of the largest markets, ripe for disruption. Sending money outside your country can cost anywhere between 10-20% of the amount. This can change with the help of *Ripple*. Banks are working with *Ripple* - A real time gross settlement system which is completely decentralized, fast and cheaper. The time and money consumed in payments & transfers, especially in international transfers is huge and painful. Other startups such as *Circle*, consume a lot lesser time and move people's money faster than existing setups for its customers. More importantly, they do not charge any fee on depositing, withdrawing, sending or receiving money from their customers. This allows them to charge a small fee up to 0.5% from their customers. This is a very small fee compared to what customers pay today and hence, a win-win situation for everyone. B2B Pay, another startup, powered by Barclays has forayed into this field. Not only startups, but big organizations like Axis bank in India have started testing Blockchain for international remittances.

The main benefits of implementing Blockchain for payments and transfers can be summarized:

1. **Real-time Transfers:** Currently, while it takes days, if not weeks to get the money across international borders, blockchain speeds up the whole process and makes it convenient for the end customers.

2. **Cost of Transfers:** As discussed above, blockchain reduces costs due to elimination of third parties or middlemen and currency conversions. This is so far, the biggest realized benefit.

3. **Serving the Underserved:** The last mail connectivity and include people into the network is something which the banks have struggled to achieve. This is possible with the blockchain system.

4. **Security & Anti-Money Laundering:** The identity and KYC management is a huge advantage with the blockchain system and prevents cyber-theft and money laundering. All information is verifiable and immutable.

While talking about international money transfers, local money transfers and exchanging own digital currencies is also a leading use case in this area.

Startups such as *Monero* and *Pivx*, which are private digital currencies and *Dash* and *Litecoin*, which make private online payments possible on an open-source platform deal with another aspect of payments and transfers.

Supply Chain

The application of blockchain in supply chain adds greater visibility and efficiency across the network to deliver higher level of control, speed & transparency to the trading relationships. Blockchain can offer a ledger, which is updated and validated in real time for each participant in the network. Real time updation will reveal asset information all times to all people and systems in the network.

A simple blockchain application in logistics and supply chain can be understood with a basic example of *organic fruit*.

The retailer understands the customer demands, say size or color or any other parameter, and can use machine based learning to predict and forecast market demand. The data is fed into the blockchain system. The supplier, who provides seeds for growing fruits, had already uploaded data about the seed quality. Each packet of seed is also tagged to identify distribution. The producer, who see this data, orders seeds from the supplier to meet the retailer's requirements and grows fruits accordingly. Each unit of produced fruit is tagged with its details such as best-before date, production location, etc. The distributors are given the reaped fruits and distributed through trucks, who are tagged with each unit of fruit and their location is traceable. The retailer receives the fruits and provides an app or platform to customer, where the customer is able to see the complete insights of this fruit (seed quality, ageing, location, etc.) and can even earn loyalty points.

More automation can be introduced by using Smart Contracts, let's say, defining that if the truck reaches retailer location (through GPS coordinates, payment from the retailer will be automatically released). If retailer's inventory touches a threshold value, set by the retailer, a preferred producer is automatically ordered for a set quantity. If the quality check is passed, payments are automatically released from the distributor to the producer.

The example explained above is very simple in nature, but should give you an idea of the practical application of blockchain and has a huge scope for implementation. The potential benefits of applying blockchain to supply chain and logistics are:

1. Faster Issue Identification: Any issue during the supply is identified swiftly due to the transparency and hence can be tackled in quick time.

2. Relationship Trust: Trusted and Open Business environment leads to healthy trading relationships and more business.

3. Automation: With the implementation of smart contracts, time and money are saved, bringing down paper-work and credit period.

4. Eliminate Errors & Frauds: The blockchain system can easily eliminate frauds and errors due to the validation procedure imbibed into it.

5. Improve Inventory Management: The efficiency of the inventory management can be achieved, by knowing the demand and supply and keeping lower inventory levels to meet the demand.

This area calls for more research and detailed analysis, and this should act as a good starting point to grab the attention and encourage you to explore more.

Healthcare

One of the most advantageous uses of blockchain in the healthcare systems is the sharing of clinical data across the various health organizations. Its streamlines medical records and this would mean more accurate and faster diagnosis and treatment. Blockchain startups such as MedRec and Gem are working in this area to revolutionize the way medical data is handled today. It is estimated that 16% of healthcare organizations across globe shall build their own blockchain systems to manage clinical data and patient records.

Although blockchain can have various potential applications, the major uses in healthcare are:

1. **Electronic Health Records:** The medical record keeping can be streamlined and exchanged within medical organizations.

2. Personalized Medication: Individual care can be provided with a collaboration between researchers and patients.

3. Drug Traceability: Using the benefits of blockchain in Supply Chain (discussed in previous section), drugs can be traced and their data can be made available to public.

4. Medical Research & trials: Researchers can use the publicly available data from the patients (by asking patients and patients will be able to monetize their data) without knowing their identity. They will only be allowed to access certain parameters, and blockchain ensures that their identity is not revealed.

This creates opportunities to simplify processes, enable collaboration and develop trust. This technology obviously promises huge potential and needs technical, government intervention and investments to ensure that people and society are benefited from this technology.

Law Enforcement

If you have followed any news about bitcoin since its inception, it is very probable that you can associate criminal activities with it. However, it is still a fact that blockchain, the technology behind Bitcoin, can still be used very effectively for law enforcement. While the technology is still at the very beginning of the learning curve for its adoption in Law Enforcement, it offers some of notable benefits.

To start with, Blockchain can be used to track location activity and store individual details for all citizens or criminals. The control over anonymity of individual's data in a blockchain is a huge advantage. This means that the information is available and searchable without requiring permissions and maintaining individual's privacy at the same time. Storing this information and spending huge money on security of servers will also be not required. In addition to this, data analytics can be used to track and predict criminal activities. Last but not the least, blockchain also reduces the time required to crack a criminal activity due to its digital nature and a lot of activities can be automated by using smart contracts.

However, this also brings some challenges which need to be addressed and agencies are already working on them. One of the major challenge is the misuse of cryptocurrencies by using blockchain for terrorist financing. Law enforcement should be able to track them down, which is not possible in the current scenario. Another major challenge is the enforcement of law for cybercrime. During a recent ransomware attack, the hackers demanded money into their bitcoin accounts by sharing their public address. This is frightening and needs immediate attention. Also, people in the past have used cryptocurrencies for exchanging ammunitions and drugs.

Handling these issues is a challenge for the government, as private agencies do not take care of law enforcement. Although it is a far-fetched situation to use blockchain for law enforcement, however, a research and insight into this area will definitely bring solutions and advantages to the governments, citizens and the society.

Voting

Another useful and near-to-use application of blockchain is in voting. Voting is a serious event for any democratic country. A transaction in this application is the casting of a vote. Because of the blockchain's immutable ledger system, the trail of casting votes cannot be altered and hence, no illegitimate voting can be done. At the same time, anonymity is maintained, which is a primary requirement of the voting system. Along with the mentioned benefits, blockchain also results in faster declaration of results.

- **Improves** voter turnout: With a minimal voting system setup, due to its digital nature, voting booths can be mobile and reach the elderly, out of country citizens, disabled or people who have movement restrictions. This will increase voting participation. Also, when people become aware of the immutable nature of the system, an increase in trust will directly affect the turnout.

l Real-time monitoring: Data can be compiled on-the-go and can be monitored by the agencies. It is a choice of the agencies or governments to disclose real-time results to its participants or not, as it may influence the people who have not voted yet. But it will definitely result in extremely fast election results.

l Cost-effectiveness: The huge amount of money spent on security of voting booths and protecting voters from the goons, can easily be avoided with the use of this system.

l Secure: As we have already discussed, the transactions of casting votes cannot be altered and hence leads to free and fair elections. This directly impacts voters' trust and results in higher voter turnout.

A startup followmyvote, has already come up with a platform to perform voting at national and constituency level in the United States and has got notable testimonials for its work in this area. To conclude, while the application in this area has still not begun, but given the simplistic nature and advantages, voting will be one of the early adopters of the blockchain technology.

Internet of Things

The internet of things has captured everyone's attention, and I would like to explain it in a manner which helps you to relate the blockchain technology to it.

Internet of Things is primarily defined by how things and devices interact with each other. When they interact with one another, we may call it a transaction. The core functionality of the 'Internet of Things' is governed by how these devices which interact with one another and then, how do they act based on their interaction. Take an example of a simple Internet of Things application, a car's engine's turns off, when the car goes out of a certain geographical boundary. Now, when the car (or its engine) sends out a signal to a server about its location coordinates, the server records and monitors coordinates' value. As soon as the server realizes that the value has gone beyond the allowed values, it sends a signal to the engine to stop working. Now, with blockchain, this simple functionality can be enhanced in the following ways:

1   Increases Security & Builds Trust: The blockchain system, will help to increase the trust between the parties (or devices) by acting as a secure system to rely on. It eliminates the attacks from hackers, decentralizes the IoT system and makes the system tamper-proof. Also, the mechanism of handling transaction, this will increase the IoT technology's adoption rate.

1   Enables Faster & More Transactions: With the use of smart contracts and real-time transaction flow, the transactions among devices are automated and their settlements are done within seconds. This ability to create autonomous systems without human inputs and making decisions on how to act based on them makes the use of blockchain a natural next step for IoT.

1   Improves Efficiency & Costs: Blockchain reduces middlemen and intermediaries to reduce costs incurred in terms of transactional costs and the device's computational power.

However, as of now, not all devices are ready to be used with blockchain and calls for further development efforts but definitely brings simplicity and other advantages to it.

IBM, through its IoT platform Watson, is encouraging the integration of blockchain and provides private blockchain infrastructure. A startup, IOTA enables organizations to explore B2B business models to trade technological resources in an open market in real time with no fees. These technological resources, which are shared, are used to operate the *things* in IoT.

Online Music

The aspect of blockchain for the music industry is that it establishes a direct relation between the creator and the consumer, removing the middlemen and third parties. Once a creator creates a piece of music, it can be submitted to the blockchain, which cannot be downloaded digitally (due to the capabilities of blockchain). This solves the ever-worrying problem of piracy. The music cannot be copied, downloaded or altered by the consumers. With the already established on-demand music concept, listeners can easily verify copyright information and pay for the music they want to listen. The payment system is supported by the blockchain system and avoids all kinds of transaction fee and middlemen costs.

Even the revenue, which takes from months to years to reach the creator, as of now, will be cut down to near real-time, which is a huge benefit. The sales data will also be available in real-time and will help to understand the consumer taste to create new music and also design marketing campaigns. This data currently is available currently on a more sentiment and abstract basis such as popularity.

Companies like PledgeMusic, PeerTracks, BitTunes, Mycelia and more are leveraging the blockchain revolution to shape the future of the music industry. Being early to dig into this new technology, these companies will definitely benefit from the first mover advantage.

Real Estate

Real estate is yet to see a consolidated listing of all properties for a given area. While this is written keeping India as a geographical area, the problem persists almost everywhere. This area has been mostly paper-driven and is yet to see a trusted digital system take over the paper-work.

Some of the huge opportunities in this area are:

- **Search Properties:** Today, we rely on property brokers, contacts and now some digital platforms such as no broker or magic bricks to search for a property. These services demand a huge transaction fee from its users, and involve a high human intervention. The human involvement may result in inaccurate data being provided to the seekers, and hence results in lower deal go-through rate and more time consumption. With a blockchain based system, the listings are open and verifiable by anyone, and will support a fee-less transaction. The data will also not be fragmented and trustworthy.

1 Due Diligence of Property: If someone has to purchase a specific property, its details have to be sought from the government's offline records. This involves huge effort and time consumption from the buyer's point of view and still the papers can be forged. With the blockchain system, given that all government records are on blockchain, any person buying a property can easily verify the complete chain of transactions relating to that property.

1 Smart Decision Making: City planning and building new houses is based mostly on forecasting and population census. With all data available on-hands, governments and property builders can use it to match the demand and supply, and city planning, leading to better and accurate decisions.

With the above key opportunities presented in this area, it is a matter of time when the governments and major real estate companies start to utilize this technology for their benefit. The government may still not be an early adopter of this, but the real estate developers can definitely explore this to create unique opportunities for their customers.

A startup Propy, has already forayed into this space, making cross-border property investment and transactions possible, enabled by blockchain technology. It integrates the ledger for the governments to ensure quick documentation (like title deeds) and at a low cost.

Telecom

Telecom in India and globally has experienced a revolutionary change recently with the entry of an innovative and low data costs player, Jio, bringing in the newest of full powered LTE technology, challenging the incumbent players against their technology and pricing models. Now, to maintain the competitive edge or to firefight this situation, it is important to keep innovating. Now, it is clearly visible that the telecom players are no longer purely telecom, but also drive a lot of services (generally known as OTT, Over The Top) which drive data usage and make use of the infrastructure and the network setup. These services include wallets, streaming services, cloud storage, etc.

The blockchain can slowly but surely, disrupt this industry. It has some of the major use cases, as described below:

- **Billing Fraud Prevention:** It has been a known fact that operators lose a huge amount of money, nearly USD 38 bn globally to frauds. This is a huge pain point, and is addressed with the help of blockchain, especially for roaming, using smart contracts.

- **Identity Management:** Since, everything is linked with our mobile number these days, from reward points at different stores to our UIDAI (for India), mobile operators possess this crucial piece of information about each of us. In a blockchain, these telecom operators can help people to monetize their personal information by selectively selling it to some partners, through the execution of smart contracts. The subscribers can monetize their information and share pieces of it, while still maintaining anonymity.

- **Enabling 5G:** This is yet another use case within the telecom domain, which can be achieved by using idle capacity for low priority traffic, innovative pricing techniques by enabling price purely based on local demand and supply and finding the fastest access node by using smart contracts. A further explanation into these use cases is purely technical and not relevant for this book.

- **Telecom Inclusion:** Blockchain has the capability to make content and data reach even the remotest of rural places. Startups such as *AirFox*, touch upon the affordability and accessibility of data

- **Marketplace for Data:** Imagine a world, where you can sell your remaining unused data from a monthly pack to a visitor from another country, who wants to buy data for a day or two. There is huge scope for monetizing unused data and also sell or purchase it without the intervention of telecom operators, who may still make money through transaction fee. The *DENT Wireless* team has set out on a vision to achieve the same.

While companies such as Verizon and Orange have already started investing in startups making use of Blockchain, it is time for other operators also, to seriously consider this as an innovation tool to maintain competitive advantage.

Challenges

It is unfair to say that this technology or platform is perfect in nature. As with most technologies, this one too has some implementation challenges. Some of the major challenges ahead for this space to flourish and develop are as follows:

1. **Scaling:** Visa handles around 2000 tps (transactions per second), the paypal network handles about 150 tps. However, the Blockchain network in its current state handles about 4-7 transactions per second. This is a huge demerit and gap from the existing systems. However, there are ongoing efforts to increase the throughput of the network and it is a major point to be addressed, if payment networks powered by blockchains are to be implemented at a large scale. The '*Lightning network*' protocol update is being proposed as a solution to the bitcoin scaling problem and once *Lightning network* goes mainstream, bitcoin network should be able to handle up to a million transactions per second.

2. **Cost of Transaction on the network:** All costs on the network are paid with the network coins. As the value of coins increases, the transaction cost w.r.t. dollar value also increases. This means that if a network charges a unit coin fee as a transaction charge and the coin is worth $5, the fee will be $5 for a $10 transaction and a $10 million transaction. Even though it would be very cheap for a large transaction, it is exorbitantly high for a small transaction. Teams are working on '*Atomic Swaps*' to reduce fee between networks.

3. **Quantum computing threats:** Normal Hashing protocols are very difficult to break as explained before. But what if the whole computing technology receives an upgrade? Quantum computing is a nascent field which is looking at considerably upgrading the speed of processing. The processing speeds are said to be so fast that these computers would be

able to find a way around normal hash protocols in today's world. Coins like QRL have already started focusing on being quantum resistant, other coins shall also consider it when the problem is a real threat.

4. **Technology curve:** The rate of change of technology is such that there may be new distributed technologies and protocols which may emerge as better options for speed and scalability. Technologies like IOTA (Tangle) and Hash graph are working to develop new protocols in this area.

5. **Regulatory Hurdles:** Various countries governments and regulators have taken a varied stance on how they view this technology and currency system. While some governments have embraced this technology, and are leading the pack with attracting researchers and technologists in this space, other countries have a more conservative view on the effect a decentralized and trustless nature of a network.

Conclusion

Implementing a blockchain requires a shift in the technology used, but more so requires a change in the process of how things work at an organizational level. When the world is moving towards open and decentralized systems, it is imperative and a matter of time when more and more organizations adopt the open culture way of doing business, creating a win-win situation for everyone. At the same time, it also addresses the very critical subject of data privacy and a matter of concern with the growing digital penetration into our lives.

While the technology and its use cases discussed in this book, help you to develop a base understanding on the subject, it is also intended to sow the seeds of curiosity in your mind to explore more on this. If you are from a technical background and interested in learning code, your next step should be to find out the best language to learn and start with it as you already know the underlying concept. In case you are an investor, you can now better understand the working and business models of blockchain based startups and how it is disrupting a particular sector. For a person looking to start a business, do something of its own or step up an existing business, this serves as a foundation to carve out a business plan and a revenue plan around it, before actually implementing it.

The world is getting smarter and hates complexity. Whatever you do, remember the foundation elements of the blockchain, which not only makes the blockchain a great technology, but if implemented with a humanly approach, will also make us a great person. All the best!

www.ingramcontent.com/pod-product-compliance
Lightning Source LLC
LaVergne TN
LVHW052316060326
832902LV00021B/3916